THE POCKET

CRYSTAL MAGIC

Published in 2025
by Gemini Books
Part of Gemini Books Group

Based in Woodbridge and London

Marine House, Tide Mill Way
Woodbridge, Suffolk IP12 1AP
United Kingdom
www.geminibooks.com

Text and Design © 2025 Gemini Adult Books Ltd
Part of the Gemini Pockets series

Cover image: Shutterstock Ltd/Sebastian Janicki

ISBN 978-1-78675-197-3

Printed in China

10 9 8 7 6 5 4 3 2 1

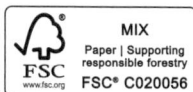

Images: Adobe Stock: 10, 14, 20, 23, 31, 35, 38, 46, 52, 60, 63, 68, 72, 75,
79, 101, 104, 107, 111, 114, 117, 120, 125. Shutterstock: Amahce (graphics);
4 / ju_see; 27, 84, 94 / vvoe; 41, 98 / olpo; 49 / KrimKate; 88 / ER_D; 91,
122 / Albert Russ. Alamy: 56 / Ron Evans.

THE POCKET

Channel the
healing power of
precious stones

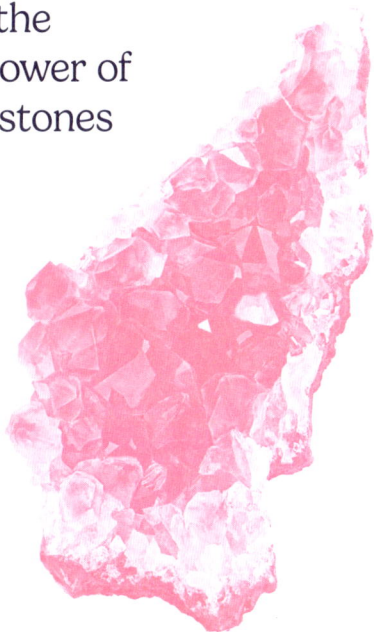

CRYSTAL
MAGIC

G:

Introduction

Since the beginning of human civilization, from ancient Sumeria to the Aztec Empire, crystals have been used as sacred talismans by shamans, seafarers, healers and warriors, for healing and spiritual use. To this day, they are cherished around the world as treasures with incredible powers to cleanse, heal and protect.

Crystals can take thousands of years to form into the beautiful gems, tools and keepsakes we wear as jewellery, carry with us and display in our homes.

Each one of these precious stones holds within it a unique vibrational energy that we can tap into to transform our own energy system, create powerful intentions and channel positive change in our lives.

Ready to find true magic? Dive in.

Crystal forms
& shapes

Crystals can be beautiful in their raw, natural form; yet many also shine (both inside and out) after being polished or tumbled.

The form or shape of each crystal will affect how it works and the strength of the energy it radiates. In general, the more natural its form, the more powerful and robust the energy; while a smooth-surfaced stone will emit a softer, gentler energy.

For crystals with an irregular shape, find the descriptor most relevant to its form.

You will also find crystals shaped for specific purposes, for example, as massage tools.

Examine your crystal against the descriptors below:

Single terminated point: Emits or pulls in energy through the point.

Double terminated points (on each end): Radiates energy in both directions.

Pyramid: Draws energy in and radiates out through its point.

Flat triangle: Radiates protective energies.

Square: Consolidates energy.

Ball: Radiates energy equally.

Geode: Magnifies and gives slow release of energies.

Cluster: Emits energy through several points.

Cut in half: Harmonizes energy, removing imbalance.

Cleansing & charging crystals

Crystals are sensitive and absorb energies. To get the most out of them you will need to regularly cleanse and charge your crystals to remove any past intentions connected to them and maintain their unique natural energies.

Clear Quartz and Citrine are self-cleansing so do not need to be cleansed or cleared.

Here are some common methods of energetically cleansing and recharging your crystals – do check each specific crystal for the best way to cleanse it.

☆ Bathe in moonlight, sunlight or starlight for a few hours.

☆ Submerge in a bowl of water or hold under running water for a few moments.

☆ Surround with or move through smoke from a sage smudge or incense stick.

☆ Perform a sound bath with a tuning fork, chime or singing bowl, letting the sound surround the crystal.

☆ Place in a bowl of raw brown rice overnight.

"Crystals are living beings at the beginning of creation. All things have a frequency and a vibration."

Nikola Tesla

Amber

ASSOCIATION:
Aquarius, the Sun, solar plexus,
cleansing, renewal

APPEARANCE & STRUCTURE:
Translucent honey-yellow with shades of
orange, red, brown; fossilized tree resin

SOURCES:
Mexico, USA, Sweden, Denmark, Poland,
northern Germany, Baltic Sea

Since antiquity, Amber has been used to heal. Known as "beaming Sun" in Ancient Greek, it was believed to have been formed by the rays of the setting Sun.

In Scandinavian lore Amber is formed from the tears of the Freyja, Viking goddess of love and beauty. Viking wives used it in their spindles, to sew protection into their husbands' garments.

In ancient Egypt Amber was known as the "tears of Ra", the Sun god. In parts of what is now modern-day China, it was thought to contain the souls of tigers, bringing courage.

Today Amber is associated with cleansing and renewal. Its luminous energy replaces gloom with hope. This natural crystal, from fossilized tree resin – some over 320 million years old – carries wisdom from the passing of time.

How to use Amber

✳ Wear close to your skin as a good luck talisman, and to keep your energies cleansed and renewed.

✳ Associated with the Sun's rays, and with light and beauty, Amber can clear "dark" spaces and auras of any negative energies.

✳ Because of Amber's immense timespan and its ability to "capture time", it can be used to encourage past life recall.

✳ Wear to boost your mood and to provide empowerment for your solar plexus chakra. It can also improve your immunity and is known to alleviate pain.

Because of Amber's immense timespan and its ability to "capture time", it can be used to encourage past life recall.

Amethyst

ASSOCIATION:
Pisces, Aquarius, Uranus, February
birthstone, yin, third eye, crown
chakra, air element, peace, spirituality,
purification, divine connection

APPEARANCE & STRUCTURE:
Purple variety of quartz; glassy lustre;
durable; large hexagonal crystals

SOURCES:
Brazil, Uruguay, Mexico, South Africa,
Namibia, northern Germany, Baltic Sea

Amethyst – February's birthstone – gets its beautiful purple hue from naturally irradiated iron inclusions. Long linked to peace, calming and spirituality by cultures around the world, it is one of the world's most widely used and well-known crystals.

This crystal is associated with the third eye and the crown chakra, leading many to use it on the journey to healing and spiritual awareness.

Ancient Greeks also believed Amethyst protected the wearer from getting drunk, with depictions of it often found on ancient drinking vessels.

How to use Amethyst

✸ Place under your pillow to produce soothing, peaceful dreams.

✸ Wear to protect against negative energies.

✸ Amethyst can activate spiritual awareness and enhance psychic abilities.

✸ Its calming powers can help dispel sadness, grief, anger and anxiety.

✸ Cleanse by burning sage and wafting its smoke around the crystal.

✸ Charge overnight under the light of the Moon.

Amethyst is the
gem for both
the 6th and
17th wedding
anniversaries.

Crystals for your zodiac sign

Each sign of the zodiac has several connected crystals, each with a unique energy that can be harnessed to bring healing and clarity. Listed opposite is one key crystal association per sign, although you will discover others as you work through this book.

Ways to incorporate your zodiac sign's crystal into your life include placing it under your pillow, wearing or carrying it (preferably next to the skin), or placing or hanging it prominently in your home (windowsill, desk or entryway work well).

You can also meditate while gently holding your sign's crystal, channelling its unique energies. You may also feel a deep affinity to this crystal – a connection unlike any other.

Find the crystal that rules your sign, and connect with its metaphysical properties.

Aries	Red Carnelian
Taurus	Rose Quartz
Gemini	Jade
Cancer	Moonstone
Leo	Tiger's Eye
Virgo	Fluorite
Libra	Lapis Lazuli
Scorpio	Malachite
Sagittarius	Smoky Quartz
Capricorn	Azurite
Aquarius	Hematite
Pisces	Aquamarine

Aquamarine

ASSOCIATION:
Pisces, Neptune, March, heart chakra,
water element, cleansing, calming,
good luck

APPEARANCE & STRUCTURE:
Light greenish blue; pointed or flat-topped
hexagonal crystals

SOURCES:
Brazil, India, Zambia, Madagascar,
Mozambique, Nigeria

Associated with the water element and Pisces, Aquamarine derives from the Latin word for "seawater" and has long been favoured by mariners as a talisman of protection on the open water.

Some believed this crystal to be mermaid loot, spilled from the treasure chests of sirens, and it is also said to ward off seasickness. Shamans believe its blue holds the sea and the sky, and use it as a tool of symmetry to look within and without.

Also associated with good luck, Aquamarine is often used as a gift between couples to soothe and prolong relationships. It supports peaceful communication, calming the mind and emotions.

How to use Aquamarine

✺ Aquamarine can cleanse the aura and deepen meditative practices.

✺ Use it for protection on a sea voyage or journey near water.

✺ Place this crystal in areas of the home where you want to bring calm.

✺ Wear against the skin when seeking emotional balance.

✺ Wear as a good luck talisman to bring feelings of peace and joy.

✺ Cleanse by burying in the earth, dipping in the sea or bathing in moonlight.

Azurite

ASSOCIATION:
Capricorn, Jupiter, Uranus, third eye,
crown chakra, wind element, spirituality

APPEARANCE & STRUCTURE:
Vivid deep blue; soft, opaque; "bumpy"
nodules or glassy with small prismatic
crystals; copper-based

SOURCES:
Arizona, Morocco, Namibia, France

Strikingly deep blue Azurite is known to spark spiritual growth and offer guidance, providing a doorway between heaven and Earth and awakening the third eye and crown chakras.

Light workers and seers use this crystal to help them intuitively read, perform mediumship and channel spiritual guidance.

Historically popular as an ornament in ancient Egypt, Azurite has been used for centuries as pigment for blue paint and jewellery, though over time, the colour fades and weathers into green Malachite (*see page 79*).

Crystal healers also use it to fight inflammation, infection and blood disorders.

Meditating with
a piece of Azurite
can sharpen your
psychic abilities.

How to use Azurite

✳ Use Azurite's metaphysical power to connect to your intuition and encourage spiritual growth.

✳ Azurite's cleansing associations can help detoxify the liver and soothe digestive problems.

✳ Wear at night to enhance dream recall and subconscious insight.

Black Obsidian

ASSOCIATION:
Protection, spiritual cleansing, healing,
success, inner exploration

APPEARANCE & STRUCTURE:
Typically jet black, also red, brown; glassy,
reflective lustre; silica-rich volcanic glass
with a composition similar to granite

SOURCES:
Volcanic regions of the world

This beautiful black natural glass formed from volcanic lava is known as the "master of protection". Almost mirror-like, it was often found in ancient amulets and talismans, worn by warriors and shamans to deflect and absorb negative energy and evil spirits. Around the world, civilizations have prized Black Obsidian for its beauty, using it for ornaments, mirrors and even tools such as arrowheads.

Now the precious stone is popular in the art of feng shui. Placed in the corners of a room, it can absorb unfavourable energies, and when set in a room's centre, it promotes stability and security. Associated with clarity and cleansing, this powerful crystal can help heal physical, mental, spiritual and emotional blockages.

There are numerous types of Obsidian, including green, lizard skin, gold and snowflake.

How to use Black Obsidian

✳ Wear as a bracelet to absorb negative energy, give protection and promote inner reflection.

✳ Using the wealth bagua in feng shui, attract abundance with Black Obsidian.

✳ For success, place this crystal in your workspace.

✳ Arranged strategically, Black Obsidian creates a forcefield to protect those within its arc.

Snowflake Obsidian

Black and white with grey patches, Snowflake Obsidian is known to purify the mind and can be helpful for those looking to kick a negative habit such as smoking.

Black Tourmaline

ASSOCIATION:
Libra, Venus, root chakra, earth element,
the king of protective crystals, healing

APPEARANCE & STRUCTURE:
Deep black (dark brown in bright light);
very hard and dense; glass-like, often with
parallel lines; compact, rod-like crystals

SOURCES:
Brazil, Tanzania, Nigeria, Kenya,
Madagascar, Mozambique, Malawi,
Namibia, USA, Russia

This grounding crystal, originally known as Schorl thanks to the German village where it was first named in the Middle Ages, has a wide range of healing properties. Like Black Obsidian, it can absorb and transmute negative energies. Its deep black colour and reflective, glass-like qualities can act as a shield against psychic attacks and electromagnetic radiation from computers and other electronic devices.

Black Tourmaline is believed to have a detoxifying effect on the body and is often used in energetic healing for chronic pain, arthritis and digestive issues. Also respected as a potent tool for staying connected to the present moment, it is believed to hold a person to the Earth like an energetic anchor.

How to use Black Tourmaline

★ Wear as jewellery when feeling low, to block out psychic attacks and negative energy.

★ Place near the entrance to your home and it will form a protective barrier.

★ For stability and grounding, incorporate into your meditation and healing practices.

★ Because of its absorbing and cleansing abilities, place it near electronic devices to reduce electromagnetic radiation.

Pink Tourmaline

This crystal is revered for its ability to help with anxiety and to promote emotional healing, particularly for those with a broken heart. It is often worn over the heart as jewellery.

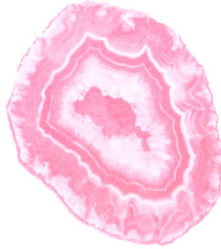

Blue Lace Agate

ASSOCIATION:
Gemini, Capricorn, Mercury, Neptune,
throat chakra, water and air elements

APPEARANCE & STRUCTURE:
Light, pale or grey-blue hexagonal crystals
with cream-coloured banded layers that
make a lace-like pattern

SOURCES:
Namibia, South Africa, Romania

Blue Lace Agate, called the "Earth rainbow" since its bands contain a wide variety of colour, has been found among Neolithic artefacts, and was believed to have been used for ornaments and healing. Jewellery and amulets have been found in the site of the ancient city of Babylon, Africa, the Middle East and Russia. The ancient Romans used it as an antidote for snake and scorpion venom.

Thanks to its power to heal and build strong emotional health, it is believed to offer "emotional facelifts". The stone is cool to the touch, which helps the bearer keep a "cool head". This crystal can also help the wearer find their voice, their truth and their power. For men, it can promote the expression of any sensitive feelings – it enhances communication and even draws in spirit guides.

How to use Blue Lace Agate

✳ To strengthen articulation and diminish nerves, keep in your pocket when public speaking or performing.

✳ Wear as a pendant, close to the throat chakra, for improved communication.

✳ Hold a piece in your hand while reciting positive affirmations – this amplifies your power.

✳ To keep the peace during a heated confrontation, have Blue Lace Agate to hand to help promote clear, concise discussion.

Celestite

ASSOCIATION:
Third eye chakra, divine energy, healing, cosmic supernatural forces, spiritual awareness

APPEARANCE & STRUCTURE:
Light blue; fragile; crystals with well-defined faces and jagged edges

SOURCES:
Madagascar, Italy – also UK, Egypt, Mexico, Poland, USA

This sky-blue crystal has ancient links with the supernatural, spirituality and healing. Legend claims it was given to Earth by the Pleiades star group. In ancient Egypt, Celestite was allied with the goddess Maat, representing truth and balance. The Egyptians used it to aid fair and just decision-making.

Its peaceful energy helps connect to the divine, stimulate spiritual awareness, and fosters inner peace and feelings of serenity. Since ancient times, it has been used for relaxation and sleep as well as to relieve anxiety.

Nowadays, Celestite is the main natural source for the element strontium, which makes the red hue in fireworks.

How to use Celestite

☀ Use to balance the third eye chakra, to improve dream recall and memory, and to heighten perception.

☀ Wear in pendants, earrings and brooches as mindfulness totems.

☀ Placing Celestite under a pillow encourages and enhances lucid dreaming.

☀ Cleanse with cool running water and charge with sunlight or moonlight.

Chalcedony

ASSOCIATION:
Sagittarius, throat chakra, peace, calm,
emotional stability

APPEARANCE & STRUCTURE:
Mostly whitish grey or brown; waxy, semi-
transparent lustre; type of quartz

SOURCES:
Greenland, Australia, Germany, Brazil,
Namibia, India, Sri Lanka, Malawi,
Madagascar

This gemstone, a type of quartz, got its name from a Greek port, Chalcedon (now Kadiköy in Turkey), and was popular among ancient Greeks. Said to be worn round the neck of the great Roman orator Cicero from the first century BCE, it is sometimes called the "orator's stone". Native American Indians also used the stone in grounding ceremonies, and it is still popular today with shamans and spiritual healers.

Chalcedony is known as the stone of emotional balance. It brings peace, calm and soothing energy. It can be used to ease emotional hardship and improve one's state of mind. It's also used for its physical healing properties, with Blue Chalcedony enhancing the immune system through anti-inflammatory properties. Another name for Chalcedony is the "brotherhood stone", for its ability to heal and build relationships.

Many other precious stones are forms of Chalcedony, including Onyx, Red Agate and Red Carnelian.

How to use Chalcedony

* Carry next to the skin to benefit from its physical healing properties.

* Sleep with Chalcedony under your pillow during particularly stressful, emotionally difficult periods of life.

* Connected to the throat chakra, press to your lips before public speaking or wear to encourage communication and integrity.

* Works well when paired with Amethyst and Tourmaline.

* Recharge using moonlight or sunlight.

* Cleanse under running water.

Crystals for love

Crystals have long been used as part of love spells, to attract love, deepen romantic connections, ignite passion or heal a broken heart.

Their energies can open you up to new opportunities and guide you to seek meaningful and positive connections. They can also be used for self-love, to deepen your understanding of yourself and build confidence and compassion.

Wear these precious stones as jewellery, or hold them to your heart chakra when meditating to attract romantic love.

Perform a simple love spell by writing the name of your love interest on a piece of paper in red ink and wrapping your chosen crystal in that paper. Place it under your pillow for one week.

Amethyst	Protects heart, nurtures self-worth, soothes emotions
Aquamarine	Improves communication
Citrine	Attracts desires
Rose Quartz	Magnifies and deepens connection, builds trust
Garnet	Ignites passion and intimacy, energizes the heart
Hiddenite	Rebalances the heart chakra and helps heal when a relationship ends
Lapis Lazuli	Promotes honesty, good judgement
Malachite	Builds trust and absorbs emotional pain
Moonstone	Harmonizes emotions, encourages sensuality
Pink Tourmaline	Removes heart blockages, heals
Rhodochrosite	Enhances self-love
Turquoise	Encourages faithfulness, compromise and consistency

Citrine

ASSOCIATION:
Aries, Leo, Gemini, Libra, Jupiter,
the Sun, sacral and solar plexus chakras,
fire element

APPEARANCE & STRUCTURE:
Pale yellow to brownish orange; steep
pyramid-shaped and needle-like crystals;
a transparent variety of quartz

SOURCES:
Bolivia, Mexico, Madagascar, Spain,
Uruguay – also France, USA, Russia

Bright and sunny Citrine is known as the "merchant's stone" or "success stone" because of its ability to bring great success and abundance. The rarest in the quartz family, Citrine's name comes from the old French word for lemon, and it is said to be "a gift from the Sun".

In ancient times, Egyptians used these golden crystals as talismans, while Roman priests fashioned them into rings and the ancient Greeks made them into ornaments. It is one of only two crystals on Earth that never needs to be cleared.

This well-loved and powerful crystal is associated with the sacral and solar plexus chakras and the fire element, promoting fresh beginnings, mind clearing, soul stirring, stimulation and transformation.

How to use Citrine

✳ Place in any corner of the house that has a melancholic feel, to uplift the overall energy.

✳ To overcome negative feelings, hold while speaking positive manifestations out loud.

✳ Align Citrine with the sacral and solar plexus chakras to help feel grounded, joyful and energetic.

✳ Keep in money trays to attract abundance in your life.

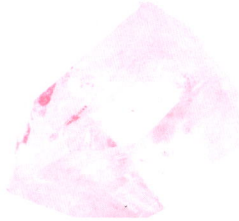

Clear Quartz

ASSOCIATION:
Linked to the entire zodiac and all
elements, the Sun, chakra balancing,
number 4

APPEARANCE & STRUCTURE:
Colourless, transparent, glacial-like; can
have rainbow hues; hexagonal crystals
with flat faces and sharp angles

SOURCES:
USA, Brazil, Russia, Madagascar, Japan

Clear Quartz is called the "master healer" or "universal crystal" and is also known as *kristallos*, or "ice" in Greek. It is highly valued by nearly every spiritual civilization – from Atlantis and Lemuria to the Romans, Egyptians, Mayans, Celts, Aztecs and Native American Indians. Its ability to focus, amplify and transform energy make it the mineral kingdom's most versatile crystal, and it once topped the great Egyptian pyramids.

Today, Clear Quartz is used in mobile phones, high-precision clocks and medical equipment because of its particular frequencies and vibrations.

Transformation, purification, cleansing, psychic abilities, healing, harmonizing and chakra balancing are all aided by Clear Quartz. In fact, it is often paired with other crystals to amplify their energy.

How to use Clear Quartz

✳ Use Clear Quartz in meditation to filter out distraction, empty your mind and achieve a deeper state.

✳ Hold a piece of Clear Quartz to psychically amplify your visualizations.

✳ Use to harmonize the chakras and stimulate the crown.

✳ Soak in spring water from first light to midday to create an elixir (*see page 59*), then use the elixir topically on skin disorders, splash on pulse points for an energetic shift, or add to bathwater.

Fluorite

ASSOCIATION:
Virgo, Pisces, third eye, heart chakra,
air and water elements, cleansing,
purifying, balancing, wisdom

APPEARANCE & STRUCTURE:
Can be colourless as well as found in
a wide range of colours; glassy lustre,
transparent; can crystallize into cubes

SOURCES:
China, Mexico, Mongolia, South Africa

Fluorite is often called the "genius stone" because of its ability to clear foggy mental states, cutting through confusion, toward fresh pathways for new ideas and knowledge. Deriving from the Latin word for flux, Fluorite creates harmony in a world of continuous change.

Fluorite is known as the most colourful crystal: black can cleanse; blue can clarify creative ideas; purple enhances our spiritual connections; pink (the rarest) opens the heart; green balances thought and emotion; and yellow aids in self-expression. Colourless Fluorite, its most pure form, improves psychic powers; it often fluoresces blue under UV light.

Fluorite has anti-viral and anti-inflammatory properties and has been used for over 1,500 years as decorative pottery tiles and cups.

Fluorite, with its
links to stimulation,
contentment and
growth, is auspicious
for birthdays,
housewarmings
and new jobs.

How to use Fluorite

✳ Wear Fluorite jewellery next to your skin to make use of its powerful positive energy.

✳ Pair with Amethyst, Obsidian and Black Tourmaline to boost clarity and focus.

✳ Wear blue or purple Fluorite to relieve stress and aid meditation.

✳ Cleanse through smudging and intention-setting.

Galaxyite

ASSOCIATION:
Virgo, Leo, Scorpio, Pisces, Taurus, Sagittarius, Uranus, the Moon, all chakras, wind and water elements, number 6, cleansing, transformation

APPEARANCE & STRUCTURE:
Deep blue-black with white, blue, green, yellow, orange and sometimes purple sparkles; opaque; tiny Labradorite crystals

SOURCES:
Canada, Madagascar, Russia, Finland

Staring into the depths of Galaxyite reveals iridescent flashes that mirror the night sky. This powerful crystal, with its fine, high vibrations, reflects our connection to the infinite cosmos, giving understanding of our place in it. It has big-picture qualities, helping us to see our soul's quest and view life as spiritual development.

It is known as a stone of transformation and change, facilitating personal growth by altering our ways of thinking, behaviour and living. It also has the unique ability to seal holes in the human energy field.

Galaxyite can dispel colds, gout and rheumatism, as well as the feelings of stuckness, hopelessness or existing without purpose. When used in meditation, Galaxyite aligns all the chakra centres and cleanses the aura.

How to use Galaxyite

✴ Make a Galaxyite essence (*see opposite*).

✴ Place over any chakra to help unlock it.

✴ Use Galaxyite to activate your entire chakral column.

✴ Use in meditation to connect with spiritual guides and angels.

How to make a crystal essence

You can create your own crystal essence or elixir by following the steps below. To use, add a couple of drops to a bath or dab on your wrists and solar plexus. Some crystal essences can also be added to water but beware that not all are suitable for consumption.

Cleanse your crystal (*see page 8*).

*

Hold it in the palm of your hand, and visualize or state aloud your intentions.

*

Place the crystal in a clear glass container and fill with purified water.

*

Leave the container in sunlight for at least 2–4 hours.

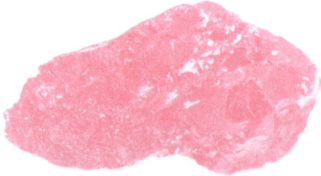

Garnet

ASSOCIATION:
Mars, January birthstone, fire element,
feminine divine, commitment, lasting
friendship, purification

APPEARANCE & STRUCTURE:
Often reddish, though can be nearly every
colour but blue; opaque or transparent/
translucent; glassy/resin-like; symmetrical
cubes with a diamond-shaped face;
hard but brittle

SOURCES:
Australia, India, USA, China

Ancient Greeks, Romans and Egyptians often called Garnet the "gem of faith" because those who wore it and did good deeds would have those good deeds returned to them; those who wore it and did *bad* deeds would have *those* returned.

This stone – so hard it was used for bullets in the 19th century – embodies devotion and understanding as well as love and fidelity. One of the oldest known crystals, it was said to lead the dead into the afterlife and lit the way for Noah's Ark.

Called the "stone of health" for its ability to purify vital organs and blood, it was worn as a protective talisman by warriors such as King Solomon, and Christian and Muslim crusaders. Healers place Garnet over wounds to speed healing.

How to use Garnet

✷ Place Garnet by your bed to give emotional balance and help you fall asleep more easily.

✷ Use to stimulate the kundalini – the feminine life force found at the base of the spine.

✷ Garnet's energizing power and association with luck can be used in feng shui to attract abundance.

✷ To foster creativity and calm, place this stone in your workspace.

✷ Use Garnet's healing energy to control anger – particularly toward the self.

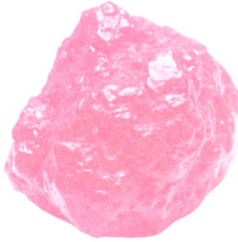

Hematite

ASSOCIATION:
Aquarius, Aries, Mars, yin and yang,
root chakra, earth element, healing,
blood, protection

APPEARANCE & STRUCTURE:
Varies from steel grey to black, blood
red and silver; earthy, metallic sheen;
rounded bumpy surface, flakes or
hexagonal crystals

SOURCES:
Canada, Brazil, Venezuela, North America,
China, Australia, South Africa

Deriving from the Greek word for blood, the iron oxide this precious stone is composed of creates red "streaks". Ancient people wore it as war paint to protect them in battle, and the famous Neolithic hand art on cave walls was often composed of red Hematite pigment.

Ancient Egyptians used Hematite pigment for the tombs of their pharaohs and made mirrors from the polished stones.

Hematite's long connection with the blood (it was also used to stem bleeding at births) means it is good for circulation, and relieving high blood pressure and heavy periods. Known for balancing yin and yang, Hematite brings the physical and energetic bodies into alignment. It strengthens the root chakra and protects empaths from becoming a sponge for negative energies.

How to use Hematite

✴ Wear Hematite as jewellery (or carry it) to benefit from its grounding and balancing powers.

✴ Use in meditation to take advantage of its stabilizing properties.

✴ To enhance focus, place Hematite in your office at eyeline level.

✴ Place in a feng shui altar in the home, for protection.

Crystals for protection

Many crystals have protective properties, warding off negative and toxic energies, and replacing these with life-enhancing qualities.

In daily life, these crystals are most effective worn on the person, or around the neck to protect the heart chakra. They can also be used to cleanse your house and ward off negative energy – place directly outside your door or in your entrance hall.

Black Tourmaline	Powerful protective sheath
Black Obsidian	Cuts through illusions
Chalcedony	Stops bad dreams, alleviates sadness
Garnet	Protects against thieves, strengthens aura, warns against danger
Hematite	Absorbs negative energy
Jade	Prolongs life, protects against disease
Labradorite	Repels negativity
Lapis Lazuli	Invokes protection of the gods
Malachite	Guards against negativity and physical danger
Moonstone	Increases focus and awareness
Onyx	Protects against enemies and passions
Pink Amethyst	Shields against psychic attacks
Red Carnelian	Drives away fear
Snowflake Obsidian	Blocks and absorbs negative energy

Hiddenite

ASSOCIATION:
Scorpio, Neptune, the Earth, heart chakra, water and earth elements, number 7, clarity, protection

APPEARANCE & STRUCTURE:
Green, light yellow, grey, white or colourless; glassy, transparent/translucent; flat prismatic crystals and elongated blades

SOURCES:
Brazil, Madagascar, USA, Myanmar, Afghanistan

Hiddenite is a distinctive, highly vibrational healing crystal. Its exceptional property is in the resolving and rebalancing of the heart chakra. This nurturing crystal allows the wearer to experience genuine gratitude, security and freedom.

Hiddenite supports you to live in a state of gratitude, to be true to yourself, and kind and generous to others. This deeply rejuvenating crystal helps clear and release emotions, bringing clarity, alignment and a higher understanding.

Hiddenite asks the question: "What would love do?" It also asks you to make peace with your past.

How to use Hiddenite

✴ Hiddenite can enhance homeopathic remedies, essential oils, herbs and hydrotherapy that focus on renewal and protection.

✴ Pass over the body to aid diagnosis of weak areas, and to promote healing.

✴ Used by metaphysical healers to treat the heart and re-spark joy and love.

✴ Works well with companions Black Tourmaline, Clear Quartz and Amethyst to heal, offer clarity and to nurture.

✴ Hiddenite can be used to support you through bereavement or the ending of a relationship.

Jade

ASSOCIATION:
Gemini, Virgo, Venus, heart chakra,
Mother Earth, number 11

APPEARANCE & STRUCTURE:
Varying shades of green as well as
white, with hues of red, violet and grey;
translucent; fine-grained, hard and dense
with microscopic crystals

SOURCES:
Myanmar, Guatemala, Taiwan, Canada,
China, Australia, New Zealand

In ancient China, Jade was known as the "stone of heaven" and was seen as a metaphor for virtue, kindness, wisdom, justice, civility and truth. It continues to symbolize luck, abundance and prosperity, and today is associated with personal wellbeing and professional success.

Energetically it enhances Qi, the flow of body energies and circulation and is supportive of the body's filtration and elimination systems.

Also known as a "stone of balance", Jade restores equilibrium to the physical, spiritual, mental and emotional planes. It is also useful for treating skin conditions including psoriasis, eczema and acne. Jade is a calming and nurturing tool that can also help us see blind spots, improve mental clarity and bring life into harmony.

How to use Jade

✳ Keep Jade by the feet in meditation to suggest practical solutions for problems.

✳ Place this crystal behind the ears as it attunes to the voices of the spirits.

✳ Use Jade in the workplace to unite a group around a common purpose.

✳ To enhance lucidity and better understand your dreams, place Jade under your pillow at night.

Lapis Lazuli

ASSOCIATION:
Libra, September, third eye, throat chakra,
water element, number 3

APPEARANCE & STRUCTURE:
Vibrant cobalt blue/violet with gold
specks; slightly dull and opaque surface

SOURCES:
Afghanistan, Chile, Siberia, USA, Myanmar

Lapis Lazuli is one of the most spiritually revered crystals across time. Sumerians believed the spirit of their gods resided within its dazzling form. The Egyptians felt it held the night sky; they carved Maat, the Egyptian goddess of truth, into it and it was worn by judges of the court. Michelangelo painted his celestial masterpieces with its ground powder; Catherine the Great decorated her palaces with it; and high priests wore it in their breastplates.

Known as the stone of "truth and friendship", Lapis Lazuli stimulates wisdom, good judgement and the higher mind. It is often used by executives, psychologists and journalists as it can reveal inner truth and promote self-awareness.

Placed on the third eye, truth-telling crystal Lapis Lazuli clears discomfort caused by not speaking out in the past.

How to use Lapis Lazuli

✸ Wear Lapis Lazuli as a pendant or necklace to enhance clear communication.

✸ Place in your workspace to reduce stress.

✸ Use Lapis Lazuli during reiki, meditation and energy work for protection.

✸ To induce a peaceful and restful sleep, keep Lapis Lazuli in your bedroom or sleep space.

✸ Feng shui places Lapis Lazuli in the north-facing parts of a home to support prayer and reflection.

Malachite

ASSOCIATION:
Scorpio, Capricorn, Venus, healing,
personal growth

APPEARANCE & STRUCTURE:
Translucent bright green, with light and
dark banding; glassy, shiny lustre; soft
and porous, with no defined
crystal structure

SOURCES:
Russia, the Democratic Republic of the
Congo, Zambia, Australia, Mexico, USA

Highly valued in ancient China and Egypt, Malachite was imported from King Solomon's mines, located in the Timna Valley in southern Israel, then ground to form part of the thick paste Cleopatra used as kohl or eyeshadow. She was buried with a vase of it to use in the afterlife. Its intense green pigment was used in Renaissance paintings and can be seen in Michelangelo's Sistine Chapel artwork. Its softness has made it ideal for carving priceless treasures around the world.

Malachite is known as the "stone of transformation" because of its ability to absorb emotional pain. It has been used to ward off danger and illness and was said to protect against falling. Placed over bruises and wounds to aid healing, it can manifest the heart's desire and give insight into personal growth.

How to use Malachite

✷ Display Malachite near a television or computer to neutralize electromagnetic pollution/waves.

✷ Use as a visual meditation tool, focusing on the swirls and banding, for personal growth.

✷ Wear when starting a new job or project, or if you are moving house.

Money crystals

These crystals amplify the energy of abundance from your aura, and are powerful tools to use when manifesting money and financial reward.

Wear these next to the skin throughout the day to attract positive energy, hold while intention-setting to increase their power, or mediate with these crystals to channel their high-abundance vibrations.

You can also place one of these crystals in your wallet or purse.

Citrine	Boosts positive energy and motivation, and attracts money and speculation
Jade	Enhances wisdom and attracts luck, encourages financial growth and abundance
Malachite	Transforms finances, unblocks prosperity and encourages smart decisions
Pyrite	Attracts abundance, protects from negative energies and remedies financial hardship

Moonstone

ASSOCIATION:
Cancer, the Moon, feminine energy,
yin, third eye, crown chakra, emotion,
subconscious, mystery, new beginnings

APPEARANCE & STRUCTURE:
Soft milky white with a rainbow sheen;
repeating layers create an optical glow

SOURCES:
Sri Lanka, southern India, Australia,
Armenia, Mexico, Brazil, USA

Moonstone is known as the "traveller's stone" and offers powers of protection, especially at night. It symbolizes intuition, balance and the feminine energies of grace, beauty and sensuality. It is believed to balance hormonal cycles and calm emotions.

Legends claim wearing Moonstone will bring visions and the ability of prophecy, while Hindu philosophy holds the stone is made of ethereal moonlight, bringing with it the faculty of serene dreams.

Linked to the Moon
goddess Diana in
Greek mythology,
Moonstone is
meant to bring
love, success and
wealth to all
who wear it.

How to use Moonstone

🌟 Moonstone can help align chakras, particularly the third eye and crown.

🌟 Recharge Moonstone in the light of the full moon, when it is said to be most powerful.

🌟 Place Moonstone on your bedside table or under your pillow for vision-like dreams.

🌟 To keep Moonstone's power close to your heart, wear it as a necklace.

Onyx

ASSOCIATION:
Leo, Saturn, yin, root chakra, mystery, love, confidence

APPEARANCE & STRUCTURE:
Black, pink, brown, orange, green or clear with alternate parallel bands, veins or spots of colour; dense, waxy; variety of Chalcedony formed of micro-crystals

SOURCES:
USA, Brazil, Madagascar, Yemen, Pakistan, India, Afghanistan, Ecuador, Guatemala

Why would Onyx be called the "fingernail stone"? In Roman mythology Cupid clipped the toenails of his mother, the goddess Venus, with enchanted arrows while she slept on Mount Olympus; they fell into the Indus River. To immortalize her body the fates transformed her toenails into Onyx, of course!

Treasured for centuries, the stone was traded in most parts of the world. Many cultures believed the stone absorbed negativity, showing a deeper black the more it absorbed. In India the stone's close and strong contrast between the layers of black and white are symbols for the love between two people. Mentioned in the books of Genesis and Exodus, Onyx was used in the breastplates of Israel's high priests.

How to use Onyx

✳ Couples can wear Onyx bracelets to protect their love.

✳ Carry a piece of Onyx in your purse or bag, to rub whenever confidence is needed.

✳ Wear close to your body to prevent overwhelmed feelings due to stress or grief.

✳ Black Onyx is considered protective and grounding when used in the art of feng shui.

Peridot

ASSOCIATION:
The Sun, Venus, August, heart chakra,
solar plexus, earth element, compassion

APPEARANCE & STRUCTURE:
From pale yellow-green to richly saturated
pure green or dark olive, can have
brownish tints; glass-like, shiny
lustre; hard

SOURCES:
Africa, Pakistan, USA, Egypt, Myanmar

Formed in the molten rock of Earth, glowing Peridot is brought to the surface by earthquakes and volcanic eruptions. The Hawaiian goddess of elements, Pele, used it as a symbol of her tears and many believe it turns the wearer's internal sorrows into tears.

Peridot has been mined for over 4,000 years and was known as the "gem of the Sun" in ancient Egypt, where priests used it to commune with the elements of nature. Cleopatra loved it for its beauty, and it remains Egypt's national gem.

Today, the "stone of compassion" opens hearts and provides protection. It dissipates hurt feelings, guilt and jealousy while stabilizing the temperament. Peridot helps you appreciate the life you have and is known to be supportive of the kidneys, pancreas, spleen and liver.

How to use Peridot

✴ Wear Peridot as jewellery, as a good luck talisman.

✴ When set in gold, Peridot can promote peaceful sleep.

✴ Place this crystal over the heart to relieve heaviness and betrayal.

✴ When placed over the solar plexus, Peridot can reduce "butterflies" and ease nervousness.

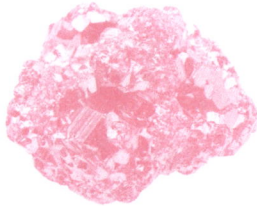

Pyrite

ASSOCIATION:
Leo, yang, masculine energy, fire and
earth elements, shielding, protection

APPEARANCE & STRUCTURE:
Bright yellow to golden; shiny metallic
lustre; often forms in small cubes or
with eight sides

SOURCES:
Spain, Italy, China, Russia, Peru

A luminous presence symbolizing the warmth of the Sun, Pyrite dispels anxiety, sharpens focus and attracts abundance.

Deriving from the Greek *pirites lithos*, which means "stone which strikes fire", Pyrite emits a spark when struck by metal and was used by many ancient civilizations as a fire starter, and even for igniting gunpowder in old wheellock pistols and muskets.

It is now used to protect properties, encourage inner strength, unlock creativity and purify spaces.

Colloquially known as "fool's gold", Pyrite may be useless to miners but is treasured by the chemical, medical and armament industries. Scientists call it the "mineral that made the modern world".

How to use Pyrite

* Caregivers and health workers can wear Pyrite to protect from disease.

* Leave Pyrite in your purse to attract wealth.

* Combine with other crystals and stones to amplify their healing qualities.

* Place Pyrite at entrances to your home to welcome in beneficial energy.

* Pyrite has a special resonance with the starting of new ventures.

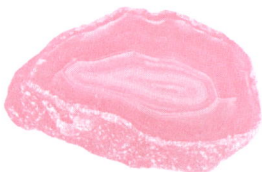

Red Agate

ASSOCIATION:
Aries, Scorpio, Capricorn, root and
sacral chakras, fire and earth elements,
protection, creativity

APPEARANCE & STRUCTURE:
Warm red to reddish brown; layered
banding and patterns; glass-like/waxy;
variety of Chalcedony, formed of layered,
tiny Quartz crystals

SOURCES:
Russia, South America, Germany,
Australia, India, USA

Red Agate has been a popular and powerful healing crystal in many ancient civilizations. It was carved into amulets by Babylonian seafarers to protect them from lightning and rough seas and its ground-down powder was used as an antivenom for snake bite. Known as the "warrior's stone", it was thought to instil self-confidence and was used in their breastplates.

Red Agate is said to discourage overspending, and help the bearer find happiness in the simple things of life. This fiery crystal of the heart chakra boosts confidence and brings fresh energy to romantic life and the pursuit of the heart's ideals. Physically, the circulatory system and blood vessels benefit from its red colour.

How to use Red Agate

✳ Place a Red Agate stone on your forehead to reduce fever and flu.

✳ Red Agate is popular among artists and writers for boosting creativity.

✳ This crystal is said to protect cooks, chefs and bakers from accidents in the kitchen.

✳ Place Red Agate in children's amulets to protect them from falls.

Red Carnelian

ASSOCIATION:
Aries, Libra, the Sun, masculine energy, root chakra, love, passion, self-confidence

APPEARANCE & STRUCTURE:
Reddish-brown to reddish-orange; glassy, translucent; can be banded; variety of Chalcedony formed of micro-crystals

SOURCES:
Peru, Sri Lanka, Thailand – also Brazil, India, Russia

Red Carnelian is the colour of fire and blood, passion, energy and life. Its fiery appearance strengthens identity and self-expression. It is known as the "singer's stone" for its ability to make voices clear and powerful.

Connected to Horus, the Egyptian god of kingship, protection, the Sun and the sky, Red Carnelian is associated with self-confidence, fearlessness and increased devotion. It is used to grow feelings of independence and spontaneous leadership.

It is an important crystal for love and the consummation of love and can help the physical body regain strength and stamina through stimulating and rebalancing the root chakra.

How to use Red Carnelian

✳ Artists, writers and musicians benefit from Red Carnelian's ability to increase creativity.

✳ Singers use this crystal to magnify their confidence on stage.

✳ Meditate with Red Carnelian to dissipate blockages in the root chakra.

✳ Wear a Red Carnelian bracelet on the left wrist to best absorb negative energies.

✳ Place atop a vision board to supercharge your intentions.

✳ Keep Red Carnelian in your bedroom to heighten romance.

Rhodochrosite

ASSOCIATION:
Scorpio, Leo, Venus, heart chakra,
solar plexus, water element

APPEARANCE & STRUCTURE:
Mostly deep crimson to pink, though can
be yellow, light brown and grey, with white
and pink bandings; transparent;
gem-like crystals

SOURCES:
Argentina, Romania, USA, Peru, China,
Mexico, Japan, Russia, South Africa

Known as the Inca Rose, ancient Inca people believed Rhodochrosite was formed from the blood of their kings and queens, and it held great spiritual importance in Andean culture. Today it is the national stone of Argentina and is prized for its ability to stabilize emotions and stimulate compassion for the self.

Ruled by the planet Venus, this rare crystal's soft pink hues make it central to the heart-based crystals that focus on love and vitality. A powerful stone, it is believed to open the heart energy centre and enhance romantic connections.

How to use Rhodochrosite

✸ Kept in the workplace, Rhodochrosite will foster friendships with fellow workers.

✸ This crystal is beneficial when paired with Rose Quartz, Pink Tourmaline, Blue Sapphire and Citrine.

✸ To meditate with Rhodochrosite, hold it in your hand, inhale love and compassion to your heart, then exhale stress and anxiety.

✸ Use to provide clarity when faced with painful matters of the heart.

✸ To open and heal the heart, place this crystal in your pocket, purse or environment.

Rose Quartz

ASSOCIATION:
Taurus, Libra, Venus, heart chakra, earth and water elements, number 7, fertility, forgiveness

APPEARANCE & STRUCTURE:
Peach or light-to-deep pink; translucent to opaque; glassy, brittle; large crystals; variety of Quartz

SOURCES:
Brazil, South Africa, India, Madagascar

Rose Quartz is called the "heart stone", "love stone" or "crystal of reconciliation". It is a mothering crystal and a love token; its soft pink hues are tied across many cultures to gentleness, love and fertility. Associated with the heart chakra, it is known to heal anger and disappointment, and to balance emotions.

Greek legend tells of Adonis and the blood of his lover (the goddess Aphrodite) mingling and staining the white Quartz pink. Ancient Egyptians believed the stone could prevent ageing, and ancient Romans used it as a seal to signify ownership and believed it could attract love. In the Middle Ages in Europe, it was used for healing potions, and in the Americas it was found in amulets.

**Wear Rose Quartz
close to the body to
help accept change
or emotional
upheaval.**

How to use Rose Quartz

✴ A large, unpolished piece of Rose Quartz in the workplace protects against gossip and harassment.

✴ To help forgive the self of past mistakes, carry in your purse or bag.

✴ Keep this crystal in your bedroom to support restful sleep and to prevent nightmares.

✴ Use Rose Quartz to reset the heart chakra, releasing stress, promoting skin health and circulation.

Smoky Quartz

ASSOCIATION:
Sagittarius, Scorpio, Capricorn, Saturn,
the Sun, earth element, security, stability

APPEARANCE & STRUCTURE:
Smoky dark-black to translucent grey or
brownish-grey hue; large, well-formed
crystals; variety of Quartz

SOURCES:
Scotland, Australia, Brazil, USA,
Madagascar

Smoky Quartz is known as the "grounding stone".
Druids in Scotland revered it as a stone of the
Earth gods and it was mined by the Celts, who
wore it in brooches and pins. Associated with
Hecate, the Greek goddess of magic, and valued
by Māori tribes, today it is the national gem
of Scotland.

This crystal promotes a deep connection with
the Earth, enabling you to work with personal
fears. It is ideal for growing environmental
consciousness and forms a strong shield against
unwanted energies.

Smoky Quartz offers security and stability,
representing letting go and surrendering old
wounds. It is a boon to sensitive people, helping
to overcome fear and depression. It stabilizes
emotions and encourages practical thinking,
leading to clear insights.

How to use Smoky Quartz

✴ Hold Smoky Quartz during meditation to help identify and let go of old behaviours.

✴ Place Smoky Quartz in the bedroom to form a protective shield while you sleep.

✴ Use to manifest hopes and dreams.

✴ Enhance your insight when using tarot and oracle cards with Smoky Quartz.

Spirit Quartz

ASSOCIATION:
Crown chakra, masculine and feminine energy, yin and yang, earth and storm elements, balancing, cleansing

APPEARANCE & STRUCTURE:
Hundreds of small crystals growing around a larger, candle-shaped crystal in Amethyst, Citrine, White (clear to opaque) or Smoky (greyish-brown) Quartz

SOURCES:
Mkobola, South Africa

Due to its appearance, Spirit Quartz is also known as fairy cactus, pineapple or porcupine quartz. Its many smaller crystals work to amplify the energies of the main stone. A spiritually uplifting crystal that has been likened to a choir of harmonious voices, Spirit Quartz tempers the self-absorbed and lonely, helping them to move toward cooperation and common ground.

Spiritually, this rare crystal balances energies, heightens awareness and activates the light body. It can be useful for encouraging teambuilding in the workplace, and in the home for fighting siblings or merging families. Spirit Quartz is also associated with protection, cleansing, communicating with higher realms, lucid dreaming and spiritual awakening.

How to use Spirit Quartz

✴ Use Spirit Quartz to help harmonize group dynamics.

✴ Cleanse other crystals using Spirit Quartz's purifying abilities.

✴ This crystal can be calming and help align the chakras for end-of-life support for patients in palliative care.

✴ Use Spirit Quartz to guide the soul of the deceased home in the afterlife.

✴ For fertility or difficult pregnancies, carry Spirit Quartz close to the body as a charm.

Tiger's Eye

ASSOCIATION:
Leo, Capricorn, Gemini, the Sun, yin and yang, solar plexus, masculine and feminine energy, courage, inner strength

APPEARANCE & STRUCTURE:
Golden brown, red, blue, green; silky lustre; quartz creates the illusion of a band of light, like the slit eye of a cat

SOURCES:
Australia, Myanmar, India, USA, Namibia, South Africa, Brazil, Canada, China, Spain, North and South Korea

Prized in ancient Egypt and connected with Ra, the Sun god, Tiger's Eye was believed to hold the power of the midday Sun – it was used as the eye in statues, regarded as all-seeing and all-knowing. In Asia, it was thought to impart the strength of the revered tiger.

Ancient civilizations used it to ward off emotional attack and the "evil eye", while today it is associated with clear thinking, courage, emotional balance, personal empowerment and inner strength. It holds onto the Sun's heat, which can help with seasonal depression and uplift negative moods.

How to use Tiger's Eye

✴ Alleviate mood swings by keeping Tiger's Eye in your pocket.

✴ Use in your home to create balance in times of change.

✴ Place Tiger's Eye in your lap during meditation to increase focus.

✴ Use Tiger's Eye in crystal energy grids (*see pages 120–121*) for protection and grounding.

Create a crystal grid

Combining the energies of precious stones with sacred patterns can be a transformative practice.

A crystal grid consists of an even number of crystals placed in a balanced, geometric pattern, displayed in your home. While you create the grid, you set an intention, which you will see come to fruition over the next few weeks.

To create a crystal grid:

☆ Focus on an intention. Be as specific as possible.

☆ Choose to lay the grid somewhere prominent in your home, but where it will not be disturbed. You will need about 1 foot (30 centimetres) square.

☆ Gather an even number of different types of crystals – try ten for a small grid. Choose crystal with energies that complement your intention.

☆ Cleanse the crystals (*see page 8*).

☆ Now, either draw out a geometric pattern on paper, use a grid cloth, or simply use your own intuition to create a symmetrical design.

☆ With your intention at the forefront of your mind, place the largest crystal in the centre of your pattern. (You can also write your intention on a piece of paper and place under the centre crystal.)

☆ Now, begin to place the other crystals and work outward, perhaps placing the crystals at intersections of the lines if you are using a pattern. Ensure the crystals are evenly spaced.

☆ When you have placed all your crystals, activate the grid by using a finger to point to the centre of the grid and say your intention out loud.

☆ Leave in place for at least a couple of days. After a month, disassemble the grid and cleanse your crystals.

Topaz

ASSOCIATION:
Leo, Scorpio, the Moon, November birthstone, sacral chakra, solar plexus, air element, number 6, protection, good fortune, peace, optimism

APPEARANCE & STRUCTURE:
Yellow, brown, pink, orange, purple, clear, green, blue; glassy, brilliant lustre; very hard, with a small electrical charge

SOURCES:
Brazil, Sri Lanka, Nigeria, Myanmar, Russia

This powerful crystal encourages optimism and creativity. Used since at least 3200 BCE, it has been known to shield its wearer from anger, jealousy, greed and hatred, and has been used as an aid in peaceful negotiations.

Because of Topaz's ability to hold an electric charge, it is thought to speed up recovery from any illness, balance emotions and provide extra mental and spiritual boosts. Its lunar associations means that this crystal is believed to become brighter as the Moon waxes.

How to use Topaz

✴ Use Topaz to manage eating disorders, regulate blood pressure, bolster your immune system, reduce joint inflammation and promote restful sleep.

✴ Wear Topaz to relieve feelings of stress and anxiety, aid anger management and to promote wellbeing and self-confidence.

✴ This crystal can work to overcome addiction by bolstering willpower and determination.

✴ Topaz can be used for protection, grounding, creativity and spiritual awakening.

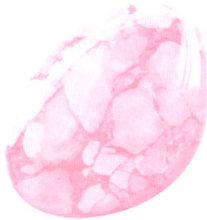

Turquoise

ASSOCIATION:
Sagittarius, Capricorn, December, throat chakra, water element, tranquillity, health, success, faithfulness

APPEARANCE & STRUCTURE:
Opaque blue-green with imperfections; smooth and waxy; tightly packed crystals

SOURCES:
Afghanistan, Africa, Armenia, Australia, Egypt, Iran, USA, Chile, Israel, Mexico, Turkey

Turquoise carries great historical, cultural and spiritual significance across many ancient civilizations. It is found in Native American Indian amulets, often in the form of birds and animals and is meant to embody the sea and the sky.

In Persia, it was used to completely cover palace domes, as it was believed to represent heaven. Turquoise, studded in Persian daggers and horse bridles, was said to give warriors courage and protection. In ancient Egypt, it was the jewellery of pharaohs, and Aztec people used it in their ceremonial masks.

Turquoise has long been used as a symbol of good fortune, health and success. Today, this much-loved crystal is celebrated for its ability to foster faithfulness and constancy in relationships.

How to use Turquoise

✸ Place Turquoise on your throat to find your voice and speak it.

✸ Because of its communication associations, Turquoise is good for writers and artists.

✸ Turquoise is a gift symbolizing unity and friendship.

✸ Worn as a cheerful colour, Turquoise can help combat depression and aid confidence.

Storing your crystals

When you are not using or displaying your crystals, it's important to keep them safe. Follow these simple steps for crystal care.

✶ Store in a dry, dark place, away from heat sources, direct light or humidity.

✶ Use natural materials, such as a cotton or hessian bag, or a wooden box. This is to ensure the crystals retain their original energies.

✶ You can usually store tumbled and polished crystals together, but it is a good idea to store raw crystals separately to protect from damage.

✶ Use draw dividers or small fabric pouches to separate crystals.

✶ There are many ways to organize crystals – from colour and size, to energy associations and chakra healing properties.

✶ Wherever you are storing your collection, cleanse the space with a sage smudge stick.